What's in this book

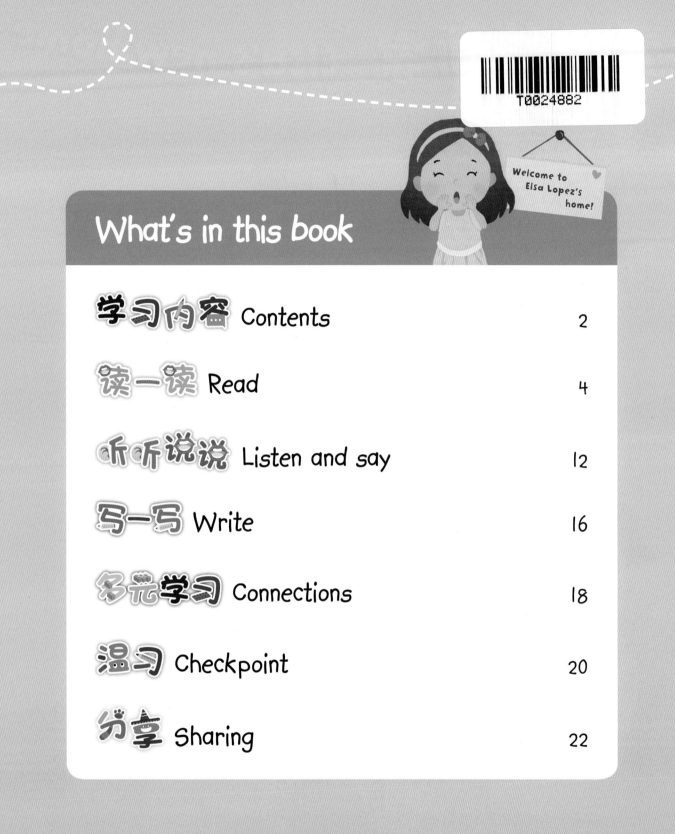

Welcome to Elsa Lopez's home!

This book belongs to

_____

爱莎的新家 Elsa's new home

学习内容 Contents

沟通 Communication

介绍自己的住所
Introduce one's home

生词 New words

★	住	to live
★	层	storey
★	着	(used to indicate the continuation of an action or a state)
★	旁边	side
★	中间	middle
★	所	(measure word used for buildings, schools, hospitals, etc.)
★	向	towards
★	门口	entrance
★	方便	convenient

参观	to visit
介绍	to introduce
号码	number
开	to open
关	to close
姓名	full name

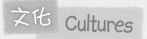 **文化** Cultures

中国的传统建筑风格
Traditional Chinese building styles

句式 Sentence patterns

大门开着，窗户关着。
The door is open and the
windows are closed.

跨学科学习 Project

设计一所未来式的住房
Design a house of the future

Get ready

1 Have you ever invited your friends to your home?

2 What does your dream house look like?

3 What is Elsa's family doing?

cān guān
参观

大家去参观爱莎的新家。下车了，
爱莎说："我们玩找房子的游戏吧！"

"开始介绍啦！我住的房子两层高，门牌号码是20号。"爱莎说。

"是中间这所房子吗？"艾文问。
"不是，要向前走。"爱莎说。

"我家的房子是灰色的，大门关着，窗户开着，旁边有棵树。"爱莎说。

"这所房子是你家，因为门口写着你的姓名！"浩浩说。

fāng biàn
方便

"你的新家太漂亮了！离学校真近，
真方便！"伊森说。

Let's think

1 Recall the story. Tick Elsa's house.

2 Which house do you like best? Discuss with your friend and tick your favourite one.

我最喜欢树上的房子，因为……

你喜欢高楼吗？

New words

 1 Learn the new words.

2 Listen to your teacher and do the actions.

19

听听说说 Listen and say

🎧 03 **1** Listen and circle the correct letters.

🎧 04 **2** Look at the pictures. Listen to the story a

1 厨房在第几层？
- a 第一层
- b 第二层
- c 第三层

2 羊和狮子的中间是什么？
- a 马
- b 熊
- c 老虎

3 要去跳舞的同学怎么走？
- a 向北走
- b 向西走
- c 向东走

① 请问买文具要去第几层？

请到第五层，卖书的地方有文具。

中间这个文具盒真漂亮！

旁边那个绿色的也很好看。

 请问文具在什么地方？

向旁边看，文具在那儿。

你累吗？那儿可以坐着休息。

不累！这里可以买文具、玩具和书，真方便！

a 坐着　b 中间　c 方便　d 旁边

1

我在外公和外婆的 _____。

2

我 _____ 的是谁？它是我的好朋友小白。

3 我们在门口 _____。

4

新年到了。上网买礼物很 _____。

Task

Play a game with your friends. Describe your home and ask the others to draw it. Then compare their pictures and see which one looks the most similar to your home.

> 我住的楼……
> 层高，是……
> 色的。我住在
> 第……层。

> 我家在……旁边。
> 房子……层高，
> 是……色的。第一
> 层有……个窗，门
> 在……第二层……

Game

Play with your friend. Choose a house, describe it and ask your friend to point it out.

> 这所房子两层高，窗关着，门也
> 关着，在黄色和蓝色的房子中间。

> 是这所红色的房子吗？

> 是的。

Chant

 Listen and say.

你的家门向着哪？
你家旁边有什么？
前面后面住着谁？
生活方便不方便？

我家门口向着南，
旁边是个小公园，
前面住着王先生，
后面有个火车站。
生活方便人友善，
东南西北都好看。

生活用语 Daily expressions

真方便。
It's convenient.

我来介绍一下，
这是……
May I introduce you to ...

1 Trace and write the characters.

ノ イ イ 亇 仁 住 住

住 住 住 住

丶 亠 门
丶 口 口

门 口 门 口

门 口

2 Write and say.

它 ___ 的小房子是黄色的。

这所房子 _____ 的雪人戴了帽子和围巾。

3 Fill in the blanks with the correct words. Colour the roofs using the same colours.

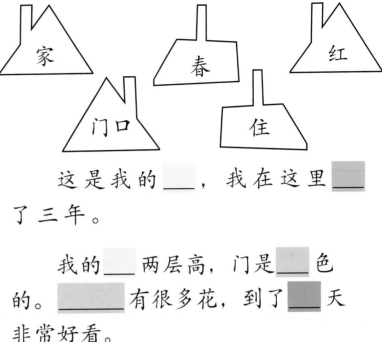

这是我的＿＿，我在这里＿＿
了三年。

我的＿＿两层高，门是＿色
的。＿＿＿有很多花，到了＿天
非常好看。

拼音输入法 Pinyin input

Write the letters in the correct place to complete the conversation. Then type it and role-play with your friends.

a 太好了，出发！   b 想去游泳吗？   c 去爷爷奶奶家吗？

"今天是星期六，我们去哪儿玩？＿＿"爸爸问。

"现在已经是秋天了，有一点儿冷，我不是很想去。"我说。

"＿＿他们的新家很近，可以走去。"妈妈说。

"＿＿"我说。

Cultures

There are many different traditional building styles in China. Look at the photos, match them to the descriptions and write the letters.

这些楼真高！

这些房子会"走路"。

这里冬天暖和，夏天凉快。

这个楼里住着很多人。

这些房子两层高。

	Building style	Chinese name	Feature
a	Stilt houses	Diàojiǎolóu	usually built above the water on slopes
b	Earthern buildings	Tǔlóu	could have more than 100 rooms in each building
c	Cave dwellings	Yáodòng	arc-shaped, usually dug out of hillsides
d	Mongolian yurts	Ménggǔbāo	round tents, built to be transportable
e	Watchtowers	Diāolóu	very tall, usually built besides lower houses

Project

1 What do you think houses in the future will be like? Design a house of the future.

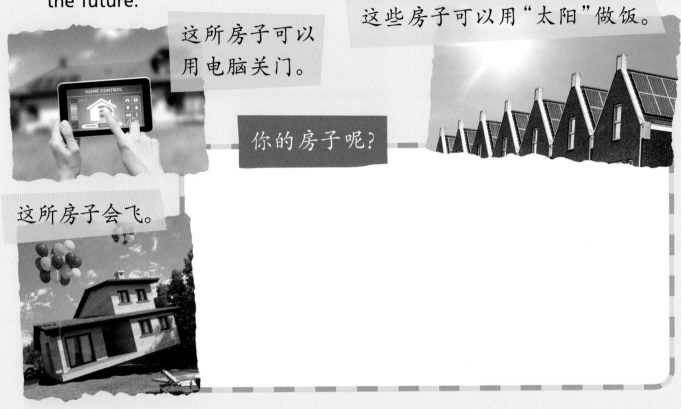

这所房子可以用电脑关门。

这些房子可以用"太阳"做饭。

你的房子呢?

这所房子会飞。

2 Role-play as a salesperson and sell your house idea to your friends. Whose house is the most popular one?

我来介绍一下,这所房子两层高,可以住三个人。住在这里很方便。冬天,外面下着雪,但是房子里面很暖和。夏天……

我想买这所房子,因为……

我觉得……

Eco-house

温习 Checkpoint

1 Read the instructions and play with your friend.

a Player A 😊 selects a number for Player B 😀. 😀 answers the question.

b 😀 selects a house in mind and guides 😊 to it in Chinese. 😊 traces the correct route.

c 😊 describes the house in Chinese.

d Switch roles and start a new round.

北
西 东
南

号码一，请写字。

❶
☐ (to live)

❷
这是 ☐☐ 。

向东走。
向南走。
向东走。
再向东走。到了。

这所房子……

❸ 他们昨天做了什么？

他们昨天……

❹ 长颈鹿的旁边是什么？

10

Ann Jones

2 Work with your friend. Colour the stars and the chillies.

Words	说	读	写
住	☆	☆	☆
层	☆	☆	🌶
着	☆	☆	🌶
旁边	☆	☆	🌶
中间	☆	☆	🌶
所	☆	☆	🌶
向	☆	☆	🌶
门口	☆	☆	☆
方便	☆	☆	🌶
参观	☆	🌶	🌶

Words and sentences	说	读	写
介绍	☆	🌶	🌶
号码	☆	🌶	🌶
开	☆	🌶	🌶
关	☆	🌶	🌶
姓名	☆	🌶	🌶
大门开着，窗户关着。	☆	🌶	🌶

Introduce one's home	☆

3 What does your teacher say?

My teacher says ...

分享 Sharing

Words I remember

住	zhù	to live
层	céng	storey
着	zhe	(used to indicate the continuation of an action or a state)
旁边	páng biān	side
中间	zhōng jiān	middle
所	suǒ	(measure word for buildings, schools, hospitals, etc.)
向	xiàng	towards
门口	mén kǒu	entrance
方便	fāng biàn	convenient
参观	cān guān	to visit

介绍	jiè shào	to introduce
号码	hào mǎ	number
开	kāi	to open
关	guān	to close
姓名	xìng míng	full name

Other words

大家	dà jiā	everybody
下（车）	xià (chē)	to get off (a vehicle)
门牌	mén pái	house number sign
大门	dà mén	door
窗户	chuāng hu	window
棵	kē	(measure word for plants)
看见	kàn jiàn	to see
离	lí	to be away from

OXFORD
UNIVERSITY PRESS

Oxford University Press is a department of the University of Oxford.
It furthers the University's objective of excellence in research, scholarship,
and education by publishing worldwide. Oxford is a registered trade mark of
Oxford University Press in the UK and in certain other countries

Published in Hong Kong by
Oxford University Press (China) Limited
39th Floor, One Kowloon, 1 Wang Yuen Street, Kowloon Bay,
Hong Kong

Illustrated by Ah Lun, Anne Lee, Emily Chan, KY Chan and Wildman

Photographs for reproduction permitted by Dreamstime.com

China National Publications Import & Export (Group) Corporation is an authorized distributor of
Oxford Elementary Chinese.

Please contact content@cnpiec.com.cn or 86-10-65856782

ISBN: 978-0-19-082307-8

10 9 8 7 6 5 4 3 2